whose
NOSE
is
this?

by
Dr. Richard
Van Gelder

WALKER AND COMPANY
New York

It is a dog's nose.

Here is another nose you should know.
It belongs to a large animal that lives on a farm.

It is a cow's nose.

Do you recognize this nose?
It is tough and round.
It can push dirt away to find insects, roots,
and seeds in the ground.
It can smell very well.

9

It is a pig's nose.

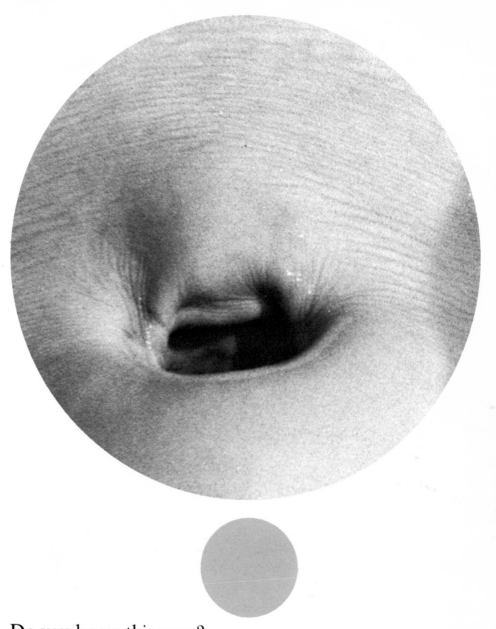

Do you know this nose?
It has only one nostril, and it is on top of the animal's head.
It belongs to an animal that lives in the water.
When this animal goes under water,
it can close its nostril so no water gets inside.

This nose belongs to a white whale.
Whales and dolphins have their nostril
at the top of the head, and it is called a blowhole.
When a whale or dolphin comes up from a dive, it blows air
out of its blowhole in a big spout and breathes in fresh air.
Whales and dolphins cannot smell.

Do you know this nose?
It also belongs to an animal that lives in water.
This animal has two nostrils at the front of its head.
It, too, can close its nostrils.

It is a harbor seal's nose.

Whose nostrils are these?

A hippopotamus has its nostrils high up on its snout.
When the hippopotamus comes to the top of the water,
its nostrils, eyes, and ears come out first.
That way it can smell, see, and hear if there is any danger.

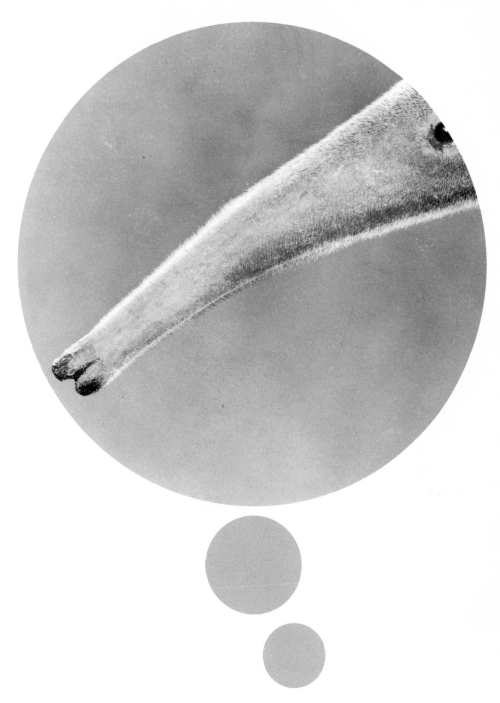

You probably can't guess whose nose this is.
It belongs to an animal that lives in South America.

17

It is a giant anteater's nose.
It finds its food in termite mounds or anthills.
With its long and strong claws, the anteater tears the mound open.
Then it pokes its long nose down the tunnels where the insects are
and laps them up with its long, sticky tongue.

Other animals have long noses.
The aardvark eats ants and termites, too,
but its long nose is like a pig's snout at the end.
The aardvark also uses its nose for digging
even though it has strong claws.

The long-nosed coati-mundi is a relative of the raccoon.
With its long snout it sniffs out insects,
fruit, and small animals to eat.

The proboscis monkey has the longest nose of all the monkeys. No one knows why it is so long or what it is used for.

The little elephant shrew lives in Africa and gets its name because its long, flexible nose looks like an elephant's trunk.

You surely know this very, very long nose.
You can give this nose a peanut.
This nose can suck up water and squirt it into its mouth
or give its owner a shower bath.
It can pull down a branch of a tree and stuff it into its mouth.

Did you guess?
It is the trunk of an elephant.
The trunk is made of the nose and upper lip
of the mouth.

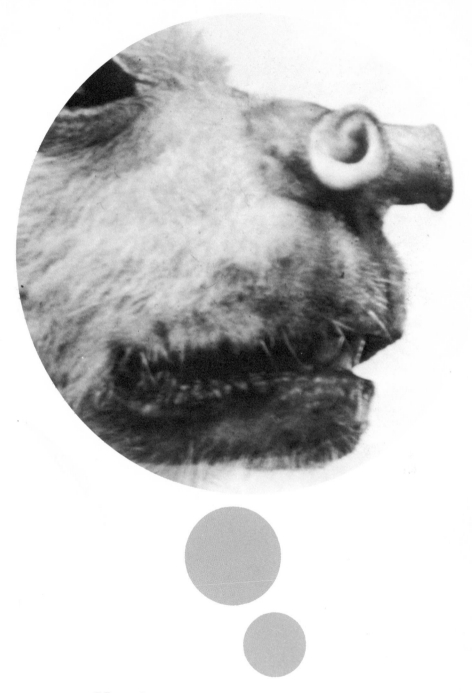

Here is a strange nose.
You will find it hard to guess whose it is.

It belongs to a bat.
Its nostrils are shaped like tubes.
Nobody knows how the tube-nosed bat
uses its peculiar nostrils.

Did you know that some animals
can blow up their noses like a balloon?

27

The elephant seal can make loud roars through its blown-up nose.
This frightens other seals and keeps them away.

Here is another nose you should know.

It belongs to a horse.

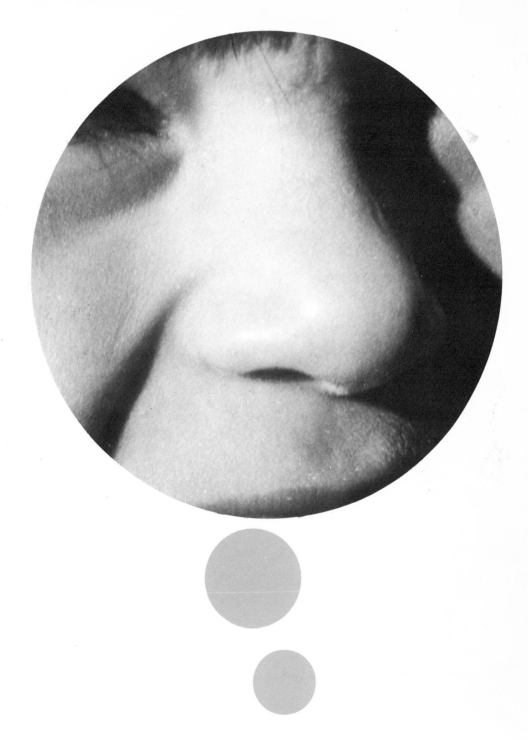

Do you know this nose?

It belongs to someone just like you.